An Analysis of Migrant Smuggling Costs along the Southwest Border

BRYAN ROBERTS, GORDON HANSON, DEREKH CORNWELL, AND SCOTT BORGER*

I. Border Enforcement and Smuggling Costs on the Southwest U.S. Border

Border enforcement is intended to prevent and deter the illegal movement of goods and people across a country's border. The intensification of border enforcement activities creates impediments to illegal entry that increase the costs incurred by migrants when crossing the border. Increased costs may include additional time investment, physical hardship, and higher fees charged by smugglers who assist migrants across the border. The impact of enforcement on illegal immigration depends on how enforcement affects migration costs and how migration costs affect the decision to migrate. Our goal in this paper is to estimate the impact that enforcement has on the price smugglers charge to bring illegal immigrants across the U.S.-Mexico border.

The degree to which migration costs rise in response to intensified enforcement can be termed the *cost elasticity with respect to enforcement*, and the degree to which the number of potential illegal immigrants falls in response to increased costs can be termed the *migration elasticity with respect to cost*. One important aspect of migration costs that can be quantified and measured is the fee charged by smugglers of illegal immigrants. Intensified enforcement activities should increase the difficulty and cost to a smuggler for getting clients successfully across the border, and this would be passed on to clients through an increase in the smuggling cost.[1] It is probable that an increased smuggling cost would deter potential illegal immigration, thus creating a level of deterrence.[2]

The degree to which border enforcement activities have prevented and deterred the movement of illegal immigrants across the Southwest border of the United States is an issue of public policy importance and has been the subject of considerable debate. It is also a challenging measurement issue with respect to both data availability and statistical methodology. In this study, we estimate the value of the smuggling cost elasticity with respect to enforcement on the Southwest border of the United States using data on the price charged by smugglers to assist illegal immigration, as collected by the United States Border Patrol (USBP) from individuals apprehended at the border, and the level of enforcement activity,

---

[1] Spener (2001) lists the key reasons for why more intensive enforcement should lead to higher smuggling cost (p.148).

[2] Interior enforcement activities also affect the economic return to illegal immigration and might indirectly influence the smuggling cost charged to cross the border. A full estimate of the elasticity of cost with respect to enforcement, and migration with respect to cost, would take into account all relevant enforcement activities. We focus here only on enforcement at the border in order to make the analysis manageable. Extension of this analysis to take into account interior enforcement, and illegal crossing at ports of entry, are tasks for future research.

---

*Bryan Roberts: Office of Program Analysis and Evaluation, Department of Homeland Security. Gordon Hanson: University of California-San Diego and NBER. Derekh Cornwell: Office of Immigration Statistics, Department of Homeland Security. Scott Borger: Office of Immigration Statistics, Department of Homeland Security. The authors gratefully acknowledge the outstanding research assistance of James Lee and Daniel Martin of the Office of Immigration Statistics. The analysis, terminology, and conclusions presented in this study do not necessarily reflect those of Customs and Border Protection (CBP) and the U.S. Border Patrol (USBP).

as captured by hours spent on enforcement activity by the USBP. Apprehended migrants respond to a series of questions by Border Patrol agents, including whether they were smuggled and how much they paid the smuggler. The data are then reported as part of an administrative apprehension record. Collection of such records began in certain sectors in the early 1990s and was comprehensively implemented in all sectors along the Southwest border by fiscal year 1999. Using data collected along the entire Southwest border on smuggling cost and enforcement hours at the apprehended migrant's crossing location at the monthly frequency, we estimate the smuggling cost elasticity with respect to enforcement.

The smuggling cost data are not without limitations. The primary concern is that the reported use of smugglers by apprehended migrants in the administrative record is much lower than the reported use of smugglers in migrant survey data, as described hereafter. Another concern is that although the number of smuggling price observations in the data is large, the percent of apprehended migrants reporting smuggling price is small. Therefore, the estimation procedure proposed in this paper will attempt to control for non-randomness introduced into the data by infrequent reporting. Smuggling costs might differ systematically for different nationalities. We control for this by limiting analysis to Mexican adults apprehended at entry into the United States. Smuggling costs might also differ depending on the respondent. We attempt to control for this non-randomness by estimating a selection correction term using the probability that an individual reports a smuggling cost conditional on whether the migrant reported using a smuggler. The probability model controls for the migrant's age, gender, birth state, group composition, group size, location of apprehension, month and year of apprehension. Our elasticity estimates are based on regression of change in smuggling cost on change in enforcement and economic factors. Systematic differences in the change in reported smuggling costs that are related to variation in reporting procedures and practices across border stations are controlled for with fixed-effect variables. Seasonality in the change in smuggling costs is controlled for with month dummy variables. What we are unable to control for in our estimations is non-random variation in the change in smuggling cost due to change in enforcement, economic factors, and collection practices.[3]

To allow for the existence of geographically segmented markets for smuggling along the border, we disaggregate the border into 12 regions, based on the presence of geographic barriers that separate regions and apprehensions data that delineate concentrated areas of illegal crossing. The empirical analysis estimates the impact of enforcement hours on smuggling costs, pooling data across the 12 market regions. The analysis also controls for change in smuggling cost due to change in economic conditions in the United States and Mexico. This is achieved by including year-month dummy variables in the estimations that pick up the impact of change in factors common across smuggling markets in individual months. These common factors include economic conditions as well as any other non-enforcement-hour factors impacting all smuggling markets systematically in a given month.[4] Finally, we control for region-specific effects by including dummy variables for individual smuggling markets.

Our results suggest that enforcement activity does have a statistically and materially significant impact on smuggling costs and thus potentially deters some potential migrants from coming to the United States without proper documentation. The value of the elasticity of smuggling cost with respect to enforcement that we estimate is in line with the estimate of a previous study that used different data and a different time period of analysis.

---

[3] For example, an increased level of enforcement may permit a higher rate of collection of smuggling cost values, or change in leadership of a station may increase or decrease the smuggling cost collection rate, and this may produce a change in the growth rate of average smuggling cost.

[4] The year-month dummy variable for month x in year y has a value of 1 for all smuggling markets in that month and year, and 0 for all other months in the sample period. We do not include economic variables such as U.S. GDP growth, housing starts, etc directly in the regressions presented in this paper because the year-month dummy variables and the economic variables are exactly collinear, and the dummy variables absorb all of the influence of the economic variables and knock the latter out of the regression. The year-month dummy variables pick up the influence of all non-enforcement-hour variables that systematically impact all smuggling markets, including economic variables.

II. The Illegal Immigrant Smuggling Industry, Smuggling Costs, and Enforcement

During the period between 1993 and 1999, border enforcement activities were intensified significantly. New infrastructure was constructed and new technologies were introduced.[5] Figure 1 shows that border patrol enforcement hours in the Southwest border sectors also increased dramatically: linewatch hours grew by 300% during 1992 to 2001.[6] The enforcement buildup led to a significant reduction in illegal crossings in areas where enforcement became particularly intense and induced a shift to crossings in border areas with less enforcement. This shift from more-preferred to less-preferred crossing areas induced by increased enforcement should have led to a general increase in the cost of illegally crossing the border. Figure 1 also shows that enforcement intensified substantially during 2006 to 2008 as productive hours rose by 36%. This period has also seen a substantial increase in construction of fencing and other infrastructure on the Southwest border as well as deployment of new technologies.

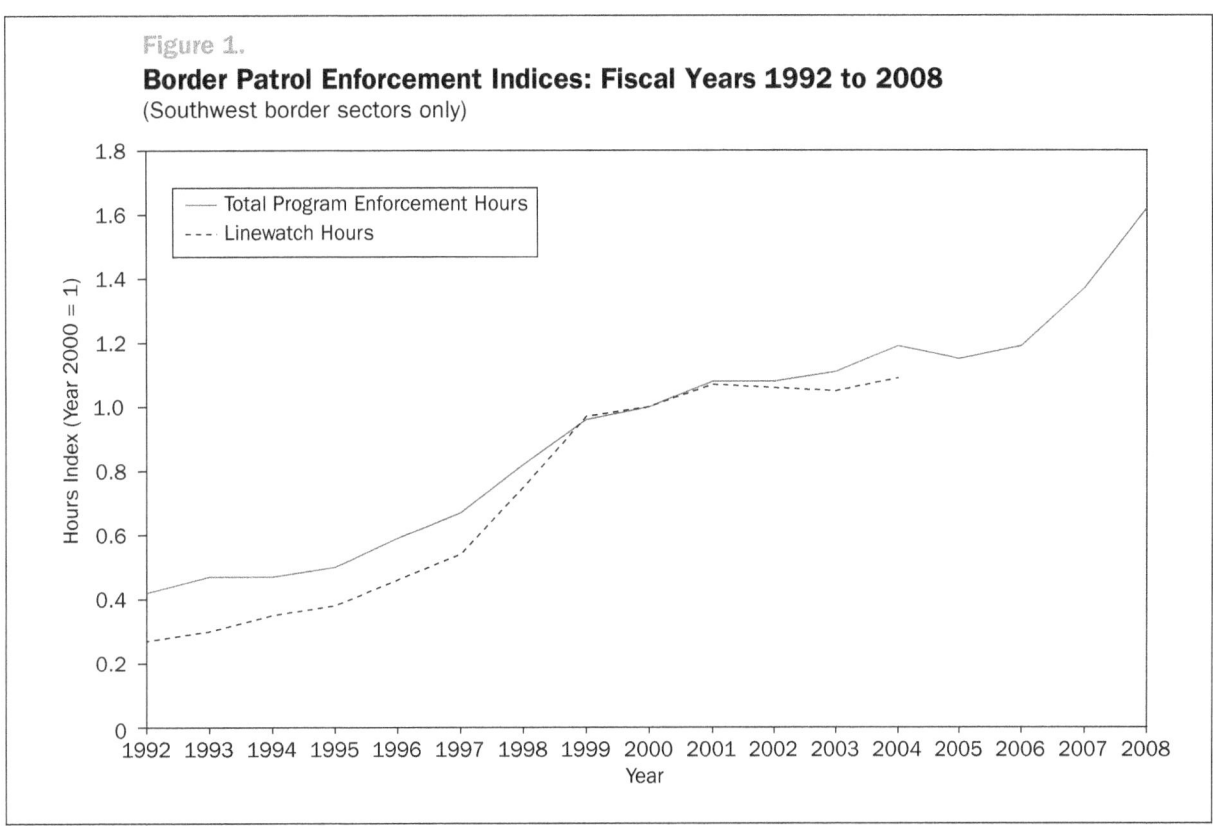

Figure 1.
Border Patrol Enforcement Indices: Fiscal Years 1992 to 2008
(Southwest border sectors only)

Data on smuggling costs charged to illegal immigrants crossing the Southwest border are available from the Mexican Migration Project (MMP), the Mexican Migration Field Research and Training Program survey (MMFRP), the *Encuesta sobre Migración en la Frontera Norte de México* survey (EMIF), and DHS administrative apprehension records.[7] These sources cover different populations of migrants but ask similar questions regarding smuggling costs, and trends in the average value of the smuggling costs reported to these sources can be compared.[8] Figure 2 graphs the average smuggling cost in inflation-

---

[5] Infrastructure was augmented through construction of fencing and roads. New technologies included night vision equipment, video imaging systems, upgraded sensors, increasing number and quality of vehicles and aircraft deployed on the border, a new electronic identification system based on fingerprints and photographs (IDENT), and other measures. See Andreas (2001), p.113-114. In addition to infrastructure and technology deployment, measures were undertaken to prosecute more vigorously and increase judicial penalties for smuggling (Spener 2001, pp.143-144).

[6] Figure 1 gives indices of both linewatch hours and productive (total program enforcement) hours. See appendix for more details on Border Patrol enforcement data.

[7] See appendix for details on these sources.

[8] The three surveys sample different underlying populations and are described in depth in the appendix. These samples also include illegal crossers who were apprehended at least once and who were never apprehended. DHS data are administrative and include the entire population of illegal crossers who were apprehended at least once.

adjusted terms for the four sources, for available years during 1993 to 2007. Table 1 provides summary growth measures for the series.[9] All sources show significant positive upward trends in inflation-adjusted smuggling cost since 1993. The migrant survey sources suggest that annual growth in the inflation-adjusted smuggling cost was quite strong during 1993 to 2000, when border enforcement activity intensified significantly. The migrant survey sources also suggest that the growth rate fell significantly between 1999 and 2006, in contrast to the DHS series, which suggests that the inflation-adjusted smuggling cost continued to rise at a rapid rate. It should be noted that the surveys have few observations in the period 2006–2008, and that the MMP and MMFRP results on the growth in average smuggling cost may change as new observations are added over time.[10]

The impact that smuggling costs have on the decision to migrate and the deterrent effect of enforcement is relevant to the degree that illegal migrants make use of smugglers. Evidence suggests that a majority of illegal crossers hired smugglers as early as the 1970s, and that the rate of use of smugglers has risen since then, particularly in the 1990s.[11] The MMP survey indicates that 95% of first-time crossers in its sample used smugglers in 2006, and the MMFRP survey shows that 80% to 93% of illegal crossers in its sample used smugglers during the 2000s.[12] In the 1990s and 2000s, available evidence suggests that the smuggling market on the Southwest border was quite "thick" in the sense that a majority of crossers used smugglers, thus making them more sensitive to and possibly influenced by fluctuations in cost.

Figure 2 depicts a consistently higher average smuggling cost reported in the MMP and the MMFRP surveys than average smuggling cost reported in the DHS administrative data and the EMIF survey. This may be due to differences in the populations captured by the surveys and DHS administrative data. First, DHS values, by definition, are reported by those who have been caught by the Border Patrol, whereas the surveys include a cross-section of unauthorized migrants regardless of apprehension. If smugglers who tend to be caught more frequently also tend to charge lower smuggling costs, then the differential between the DHS series and the MMP and MMFRP series could be explained at least in part by the fact that the latter include more values for higher-quality smugglers.[13] Second, the MMP and MMFRP surveys have a greater percent of their sample populations crossing the border in the San Diego sector. The smuggling costs in San Diego are reported as higher than other crossing locations and therefore could account for the difference between the reported smuggling cost series. Third, there may be systematic differences in the nature of smuggling services whose price is reported to DHS versus the surveys.[14]

---

[9] Real smuggling cost is nominal smuggling cost in US dollars deflated by the US consumer price index.

[10] The most recent available MMP data has a total number of smuggling cost observations of 7, 2, and 0 in 2006, 2007, and 2008 respectively (average annual number of observations in 2000-2005 was 48.) The most recent MMFRP data has 23, 11, and 6 observations in 2006, 2007, and 2008 respectively (average annual number of observations in 2000-2005 was 45.) The MMP and MMFRP surveys ask migrant households about their immigration history, so that in a given survey year, information on trips taken prior to that year is collected and added to the survey database. As new waves of interviews are done, the number of observations for historical years will increase.

[11] A survey of illegal immigrants who legalized through the IRCA program of the late 1980s suggests that in the late 1970s-early 1980s, 59% of Mexican nationals who entered the U.S. illegally used a smuggler (see Immigration Reform and Control Act: Report on the Legalized Alien Population, U.S. Department of Justice, Immigration and Naturalization Service, March 1992). Spener (2005) reviews other evidence that suggests that 40% to 50% of illegal crossers used smugglers in the first half of the 1970s (pp.45–46.) For the period 1965 to 1994, MMP data suggests that for all undocumented crossers in the sample, 68% of trips were made with smuggler assistance (Orrenius 1999, p.12). The MMP survey also suggests that use of a smuggler by first-time crossers rose from 80% to 90% between 1990 and 1999. Using results from several small surveys of illegal crossers in the 1980s and 1990s, Lopez-Castro (1997) concludes that roughly 70–80% of illegal crossers used smugglers.

[12] For the MMP survey, see http://mmp.opr.princeton.edu/results/002coyote-en.aspx. The MMFRP survey covers three Mexican towns: 93% of crossers from Tlacuitapa used smugglers during 2000 to 2006, 90% from Tunkas used smugglers during 2000 to 2009, and 80% from San Miguel Tlacotepec used smugglers during 2000 to 2007.

[13] The underlying populations also differ in that the MMFRP samples crossers in three Mexican towns and the MMP in rural communities that are traditional sources of immigrants, whereas EMIF and DHS sample crossers along the full length of the border. Comparison of DHS average smuggling cost for apprehended crossers from the birth states in which the MMFRP towns are located with relevant MMFRP values show that MMFRP values are significantly above DHS values even after controlling for this.

[14] For example, apprehended migrants may tend to more frequently report the price paid to smugglers to get to the border as opposed to the full smuggling price for the entire trip.

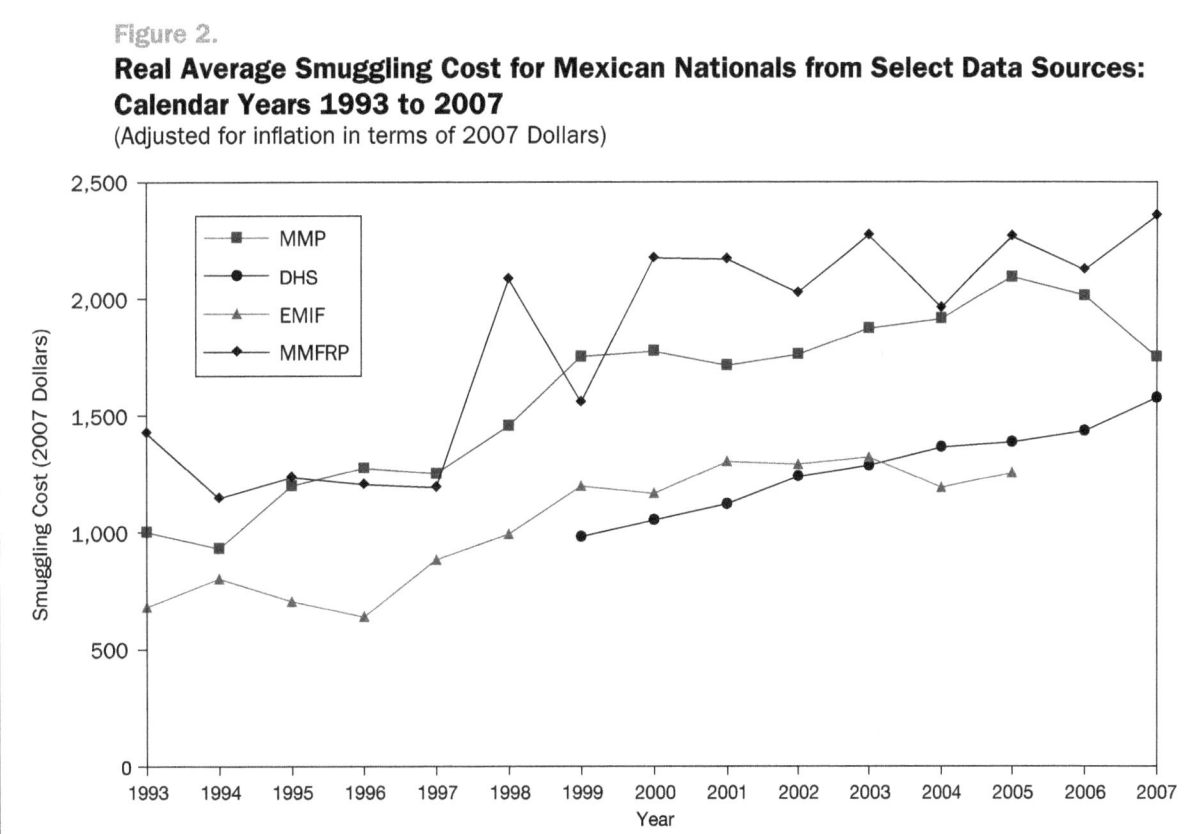

Figure 2.

Real Average Smuggling Cost for Mexican Nationals from Select Data Sources: Calendar Years 1993 to 2007

(Adjusted for inflation in terms of 2007 Dollars)

Source: Mexican Migration Project (MMP); Department of Homeland Security, ENFORCE; Encuesta sobre Migración en la Frontera Norte de México survey (EMIF); and Mexican Migration Field Research and Training Program survey (MMFRP).

Table 1.

Smuggling Costs Summary Statistics by Data Source: Calendar Years 1993 to 2006

Data source	Average smuggling cost for Mexican nationals	Average annual growth of real smuggling costs:		
		1993–2006	1993–2000	2000–2006
DHS ENFORCE	$1,305	NA	NA	5.3%
EMIF survey	$1,182	5.2%[A]	8.0%	1.5%[A]
MMP survey	$1,970	5.5%	8.5%	2.1%
MMFRP survey	$1,845	3.1%	6.2%	−0.4%

NA Not Available.

[A]Average annual growth during 1999 to 2005.

Note: Average smuggling cost values are for 2005 and are unweighted averages of individual survey or apprehension record values. DHS, EMIF, and MMP averages include values for many crossing sites along the length of the Southwest border. MMRFP average includes smuggling cost values for illegal crossers from three Mexican towns (Tlacuitapa, Tunkas, and San Miguel Tlacotepec.) For DHS and MMFRP, smuggling costs for illegal crossers who entered between ports of entry only are included. For EMIF and MMP, smuggling costs for all types of illegal crossers are included.

Source: U.S. Department of Homeland Security, Enforcement Case Tracking System (ENFORCE); Encuesta sobre Migración en la Frontera Norte de México survey (EMIF); Mexican Migration Project (MMP); and Mexican Migration Field Research and Training Program survey (MMFRP). MMP, MMFRP, and EMIF surveys: calculated using raw data of the surveys.

The sustained rise in the inflation-adjusted smuggling cost over the past 15 years and the increased rate of smuggler use is suggestive that border enforcement activity has increased the cost of illegally crossing into the United States and thus potentially deterred illegal immigration. However, smuggling costs may have risen due to increased demand for smugglers resulting from a rapidly rising flow of illegal crossers. Given this possibility, it is necessary to analyze the impact of enforcement on smuggling costs in the context of supply of and demand for smuggling services in order to accurately estimate an elasticity of smuggling cost with respect to enforcement.

Previous research suggests that intensified border enforcement as captured by Border Patrol linewatch hours has significant impacts on apprehensions and smuggling costs, and may have had a deterrence impact on the inflow of illegal immigrants. Hanson and Spilimbergo (1999) analyze the level of apprehensions on the Southwest border during 1963 to 1996 and find that apprehensions are significantly influenced by both economic and enforcement variables. A 10% reduction in Mexican wages relative to U.S. wages results in a 6% increase in border apprehensions.[15] Angelucci (2005) uses data on individual illegal migration experiences from the Mexican Migration Project (MMP) for the period 1972 to 1993 and analyzes the relationship between inflows and outflows of illegal migrants and economic and enforcement variables. She finds that both economic and enforcement variables have statistically and quantitatively significant impacts on illegal migration inflow. She also finds that increased enforcement reduced outflow of illegal migrants and increased the duration of stay in the United States, so that the net stock of illegal immigrants resident in the United States may have risen. Orrenius and Zavodny (2005) analyze the likelihood of a male Mexican national making an illegal trip to the United States during 1965 to 1996 using MMP data and find that enforcement intensification has a negative but statistically insignificant impact on the decision to migrate illegally. These studies do not explicitly analyze smuggling costs, how they are affected by enforcement, and how these costs affect the migration decision.

Other recent works address smuggling costs directly. Orrenius (1999) uses MMP data on individual migration experiences of male Mexican household heads for the period 1965 to 1994 to evaluate the relationship between the decision to migrate, economic variables, and variables that affect the cost of migrating (smuggling costs and network effects). She finds that an increase in smuggling costs significantly negatively affects the likelihood of migration, thus producing a deterrent effect. Gathmann (2008) explicitly models the illegal migration decision including the possibility of hiring a smuggler and uses MMP data on individual migration experiences for the period 1972 to 2003 to estimate the smuggling cost elasticity with respect to enforcement, and the migration decision elasticity with respect to enforcement. She finds that the elasticity of smuggling costs with respect to enforcement was statistically significant and equal to 0.25, so that a 10% increase in enforcement hours resulted in a 2.5% increase in smuggling costs.[16] She also finds that increased enforcement has a negative but statistically insignificant impact on the decision to migrate illegally.[17] Carrion-Flores and Sorenson (2006) use MMP data to estimate a model of choice by an illegal crosser that captures both deterrence and diversion impacts of enforcement and find that both impacts were significant.

We contribute to this literature on the deterrence impact of border enforcement activities by using DHS apprehension record data to estimate the impact of enforcement as proxied by Border Patrol enforcement hours on smuggling costs. Before moving to our estimation strategy and results, it will be useful to review what is known about the nature of the migrant smuggling industry on the Southwest border.

III. Supply and Demand in the Smuggling Industry

Demand for smuggling services is primarily driven by the need for illegal crossers to access the expertise, knowledge, equipment, and other assets of smugglers. Total demand for smuggler services is influenced by the total number of illegal crossers seeking such services, which is affected by economic conditions in Mexico and the United States, the cost of smuggling services, and the cost of alternative methods of entering the United States. The choice of where to cross the border will also be affected by

---

[15] Hanson and Spilimbergo use the average Mexican wage in the manufacturing sector and use U.S. wage data to construct a U.S. wage most relevant for a prospective Mexican migrant.

[16] Gathmann estimates two elasticities of smuggling costs with respect to enforcement: the elasticity of smuggling costs charged to illegal crossers in a particular Border Patrol sector with respect to enforcement in that particular sector, and the elasticity with respect to enforcement in neighboring sectors. The former elasticity value is 0.25, and the latter is 0.24. These values suggest that a 10% increase in enforcement in a sector results in a 2.5% increase in smuggling costs in that sector as well as in neighboring sectors.

[17] Gathmann does not estimate an elasticity of the migration decision with respect to smuggling costs.

how high the smuggling cost charged by smugglers operating in that area is compared to other areas. The supply of smuggling services is influenced by how difficult and risky it is for smugglers to operate in a given area, which in turn is impacted by the intensity of enforcement, judicial policies regarding apprehended smugglers, nature of terrain, and the experience and knowledge of the smuggler. Smuggling costs will also be influenced by the degree of competitiveness in the smuggling market. If one large smuggling operation monopolizes a particular area, it might set smuggling costs at a high level to maximize its profits. An increasing number of operations in the market will lead to greater competition and a lower price.

The smuggling industry is characterized by significant differentiation with respect to suppliers and products. López Castro (1997) uses results from several surveys of smugglers, unauthorized migrants, and INS investigators to describe an industry with several distinct smuggler types: local smugglers who live in the same hometown or region of the crosser, local-border smugglers who live near the border but are from the hometown or region of the migrants, and border-business smugglers who assemble groups of migrants at the border. Each relationship involves a different set of benefits and risks for the migrants and the smugglers.[18] A common theme in the analysis of the smuggling industry over the past three decades is that as enforcement has intensified, smaller smuggling operations have been squeezed out of the industry and larger, better-funded operations have expanded, and that the latter have a greater tendency to violate terms of agreement with crossers and abuse them or abandon them in the course of a trip.[19] Other analysts contend that various incentives serve to keep such abuses in check and that the consolidation of the industry into larger operations over time has been exaggerated.[20] If the smuggling industry was becoming less competitive over time, smuggling costs may have risen due to more powerful cartel-like operations taking advantage of their increased market power to raise price. Empirical data that would permit evaluation of the degree to which this may have been happening over time is lacking.

The smuggling industry also offers a range of services to illegal crossers. Some crossers pay for a very short trip from one bank of the Rio Grande River to the other, while others pay for passage from their hometown in central or southern Mexico to a final destination city in the north of the United States. Although smuggling costs will depend on how far the final destination is from the border, and how many checkpoints must be traversed to reach the destination, available data sources on smuggling costs do not provide information that permits controlling for such product differentiation.[21] The smuggling industry is also characterized by price discrimination. Personal characteristics of individual migrants can affect the smuggling cost charged. Previous research suggests that women are typically charged higher fees than men (especially pregnant women), and that age can also influence the price.[22] Based on apprehensions data, there is substantial variation in the size of smuggled groups that are caught by the Border Patrol. Price appears to vary with group size, perhaps reflecting differences in apprehension probabilities for groups based on their number and composition of members.

Finally, the smuggling industry might be characterized by economies of scope for smugglers such that they can lower the smuggling cost charged by combining different types of business activities. The most obvious example is combining human and drug smuggling. Available evidence on the degree to which these two smuggling activities are combined is very scant.[23]

---

[18] See also Spener (2001) for a review of smuggler types in the south Texas area.

[19] For example, Andreas (2001) argues that rapidly increasing flows and enforcement intensification in the 1970s and the 1990s led to such a shift in smuggling operations (p.110 and pp.117–118.)

[20] Spener (2001, 2004) summarizes this point of view and argues that smugglers usually have incentives to honor agreements with clients in order to not damage their reputation and lose future business, avoid denunciation by clients to the Border Patrol upon apprehension, and receive payment when they are paid only after successfully delivering clients to final destinations. The "cash-on-delivery" payment approach is apparently used extensively in today's smuggling industry and may have been common back to the 1970s (see Fuentes and Garcia 2009, pp.87–89, and Spener 2005, pp.62–64). Fuentes and Garcia note that in some cash-on-delivery arrangements, the crosser is unaware of the smuggling fee being paid because smugglers deal only with the person's family or friends in the US who are paying for the trip (p.87).

[21] Fuentes and Garcia (2009) give empirical examples of how smuggling cost varies with length of trip (pp.96–97). Spener (2001) lists a menu of specific services offered by smugglers of Mexican crossers in the south Texas area (p.134–135)

[22] See, for example, Fuentes and Garcia (2009), pp.94–96.

[23] Fuentes and Garcia (2009), pp.97–98, discuss this issue.

Our approach is to treat smuggling operations as profit maximizing firms that compete with one another for business. Given the expanse of the Southwest border region, it is natural to imagine that markets for smuggling services are spatially segmented, with smugglers tending to focus on particularly geographic regions. Migrants, by seeking the lowest price and best services, are likely to arbitrage price differences across individual smuggling markets, making the price in one location sensitive to a change in conditions at another location. We explicitly allow for such interaction across locations in the empirical analysis.

IV. Empirical Analysis of Smuggling Costs, Enforcement, and Economic Factors

A Conceptual Model of Migration and Smuggling

To motivate the empirical analysis, it is helpful to begin with a conceptual model of the market for migrant smuggling. Consider the pool of potential migrants in Mexico. Each month, imagine that some fraction of the Mexican population considers migrating to the United States. Each potential migrant compares the expected wage in the United States, less the cost of crossing the border and any disamenity associated with migration, against the expected wage in Mexico. The larger the U.S.-Mexico wage difference and the smaller the border crossing cost, the more likely it is that individuals will decide to cross the border.

Once individuals choose to cross the border, they select a crossing site. The choice will depend on the price that smugglers charge to cross the border at each potential site (the smuggling cost), as well as characteristics of locations that are unrelated to economic conditions (climate, topography, distance from their home in Mexico, proximity to desired U.S. destination). Econometrically, we summarize the factors that determine how many individuals choose a particular location as consisting of the local smuggling cost (which varies by location and time), the average smuggling cost across all crossing sites (which varies by time but not by location), economic conditions in the United States and Mexico (which vary by time but not by location), and fixed conditions at a site (which varies by location but not time). In the estimation, we will control for time period "fixed effects," which will neutralize the impact of average conditions along the border and general economic conditions in the United States and Mexico, and location "fixed effects," which will neutralize the impact of fixed location characteristics. This approach allows us to estimate the impact of enforcement on the smuggling cost, while controlling for a wide range of factors (whether observed or unobserved) that affect the smuggling market.

What determines the smuggling cost? Imagine a market for smuggler services in which smugglers differentiate their services by focusing on particular locations along the border. After investing in acquiring and protecting their "turf," they control smuggling over some stretch of the border. If we imagine that the amount of territory any individual smuggler can control is relatively small relative to the entire expanse of the border, then we will have a market equivalent to monopolistic competition: each smuggler exerts market power over his territory but also faces competition from many other smugglers in other locations. The local market power smugglers enjoy allows them to charge a price that is a markup over their marginal cost of providing smuggling services. Smugglers may then earn profits, unless sufficient smugglers enter to drive these profits to zero. Costs borne by smugglers, in turn, are a function of the expense of hiring guides (which will depend on labor market conditions in the United States and Mexico), the features of the terrain (climate topography, distance from Mexican and U.S. cities), and, most importantly, the costs associated with enforcement against illegal entry by the U.S. Border Patrol. Higher enforcement means higher risk of capture, requiring smugglers to increase the wages they pay guides (either as compensation for risk of arrest or for the greater amount of time it takes to evade capture during a crossing).

Will the smuggling price depend on the volume of migrants who wish to cross the border? The answer is unclear. As demand for smugglers increases, more smugglers will choose to enter the market, accommodating the extra crossers, meaning that the volume of migrants per smuggler may not change all that much even if the aggregate volume of crossers swings widely. Entry by smugglers serves to eliminate extra profits caused by a demand rise and exit by smugglers serves to eliminate losses causes by a demand fall. For changes in crossing volume to affect the price, volume would have to affect the costs that individual smugglers incur for running their business. For instance, a surge in demand for crossing may lead to an increase in demand for guides, driving up their wages and, because the smuggler price is a markup over cost, the price that smugglers charge. But this would require the supply of guides to be somewhat inelastic. While price increases associated with rising guide prices might exist in the short turn, it is unlikely they would persist in the long run, owing to the large supply of available labor in Mexico.

The conceptual model suggests an econometric specification that has the smuggling price at a specific location as a function of Border Patrol enforcement at that location, Border Patrol enforcement at other locations, economic conditions in the United States and Mexico (which affect the cost of hiring guides either through affecting volume or the alternative wage of guides), and the fixed characteristics of a site (associated with geography and climate). For the empirical analysis, we need measures of the smuggler price and border enforcement and controls for economic conditions and location characteristics. Because economic conditions are assumed to be common to all locations along the border, we will control for them by including dummy variables for the time period in the analysis (the number of dummy variables included equals n-1, where n is the number of months in the sample). And because location characteristics are fixed, we will control for them by controlling for location dummy variables (where the number of dummies equals the number of smuggling markets).

Data on Smuggling Costs and Enforcement

The analysis focuses on individuals from Mexico attempting to enter the United States. While Border Patrol data report apprehensions for many non-Mexicans, there are insufficient data for other countries to support meaningful empirical analysis. We limit the sample to individuals who (a) report that they were Mexican citizens, (b) were apprehended between ports of entry by Border Patrol agents (patrolling the border) whose stations are in the territory adjacent to Mexico, and (c) were arrested at entry.

The data the Border Patrol collects on smuggling costs were collected in certain sectors in the early 1990s and collected in all sectors along the Southwest border by fiscal year 1999. However, in the initial years of the border-wide data collection, very few of the individuals apprehended reported information on smuggling. Table 2 reports the percentage of individuals in our sample (i.e., subject to the sample restrictions (a)-(c) described above) who either report the use of a smuggler or report a positive smuggling cost. The reported use of a smuggler rises from 3.2% in 1999 to 20.4% in 2003 and then fluctuates thereafter. The proportion reporting a positive smuggling cost rises from 0.9% in 1999 to 6.5% in 2005 and fluctuates thereafter. The percentage of apprehended individuals who report use of a smuggler in DHS apprehension records is far smaller than the proportion reported by surveys.[24]

Table 2.

Percent of Border Patrol Apprehensions that Reported use of a Smuggler and Cost: Fiscal Years 1999 to 2008

	Percent of apprehended individuals reporting:	
Year	Use of Smuggler	Smuggling Cost
1999	3.2	0.9
2000	4.3	1.3
2001	7.9	2.0
2002	11.2	2.9
2003	20.4	4.0
2004	23.6	5.6
2005	16.9	6.5
2006	15.3	6.9
2007	16.0	6.1
2008	18.0	6.5

Source: U.S. Department of Homeland Security, ENFORCE.

[24] Survey evidence reviewed in section II above suggests that a large majority of crossers used smugglers in the 2000s. Those apprehended by the Border Patrol often have incentives to not report being smuggled even when they are using a smuggler. See section on DHS apprehension records in appendix on data sources for further discussion.

Because of missing data in 1999, we exclude this year from the analysis. In all other results, we report estimates either for 2000 to 2008, which we refer to as the full sample period, or for the period 2002 forward, a shorter period for which we have more complete data.

To perform the analysis, we need to define smuggling markets. There are 46 Border Patrol stations and headquarter stations whose territory adjoins the U.S. border with Mexico. These stations appear to be too disaggregated to represent individual smuggling markets. In the San Diego Sector, for instance, the Imperial Beach, Brown Field, and Chula Vista Stations are within the San Diego metropolitan area and have no physical barriers separating them. Because of the lack of geographic barriers, we treat these stations as a single market. Moving east, one encounters a mountainous region in which the El Cajon, Campo/Pine Valley, and Boulevard Stations are located, which we treat as a second market, before entering the flat and open Imperial Valley, in which the El Centro and Calexico Stations are located, which we treat as a third market.

We continue along the border, defining nine additional markets, three in Texas (McAllen, which is most of the lower Rio Grande Valley; Laredo, which is most of the upper Rio Grande Valley; and El Paso East, which is a lightly travelled and mostly mountainous region, including the Big Bend area), one in New Mexico (El Paso West, which includes the expansive area west of El Paso), and five in Arizona (Tucson East, Sonoita, Tucson, Tucson West, and Yuma—each of which are divided by mountainous and/or desert stretches of one kind or another). The smuggling markets and the Border Patrol stations assigned to them are described in Table 3. The only market occupied by a single station is Sonoita, which is a high traffic area separated by mountains from Border Patrol stations to the east and west. Given the small sample sizes in some Border Patrol stations, it would be difficult to conduct the analysis for smuggling markets divided geographically much more finely that the 12 regions in Table 3.

Table 3.

Border Patrol Stations in Each Smuggling Market along the Southwest Border

Smuggling market	Border Patrol Station	Smuggling market	Border Patrol Station
McAllen, TX	Brownsville	El Paso, TX West	Deming
	Fort Brown		Lordsburg
	Harlingen		Santa Teresa
	McAllen	Tucson, AZ East	Douglas
	Weslaco		Naco
	Rio Grande City	Sonoita	Sonoita
Laredo, TX	Laredo North	Tucson	Nogales
	Laredo South		Tucson
	Zapata	Tucson, AZ West.	Ajo
	Brackettville		Casa Grande
	Comstock	Yuma, AZ	Wellton
	Del Rio		Yuma
	Eagle Pass	El Centro, CA	Calexico
	Sanderson		El Centro
El Paso, TX East	Alpine	San Diego, CA West	Imperial Beach
	Marfa		Brown Field
	Presidio		Chula Vista
	Sierra Blanca	San Diego, CA East	Campo
	Van Horn		El Cajon
	El Paso		
	Fabens		
	Fort Hancock		
	Ysleta		

Note: Smuggling markets defined by authors based on geographic barriers within sectors.

Figure 3 lists the number of observations by month for each of the 12 geographic smuggling markets previously described. Note that we have fewer observations (less than 150 per month) for El Paso East, McAllen, San Diego West, and Tucson East. The differences in the reported observations in the data could be the result of either a limited number of total apprehensions due to the remoteness of the market (El Paso East, Tucson East), or differences in reporting frequencies at the sector and station level. The former difference in observations could increase the importance of small smuggling markets in the estimate of the impact of enforcement on smuggling costs. The latter difference in observations across smuggling markets introduces non-randomness in the data collection. We control for any non-randomness in the data collection by using a sample selection bias treatment procedure described hereafter. Moreover, we will examine whether the results are sensitive to weighting the estimates by sample size, weighting the estimates by the share of apprehensions or dropping the regions with the least number of observations.

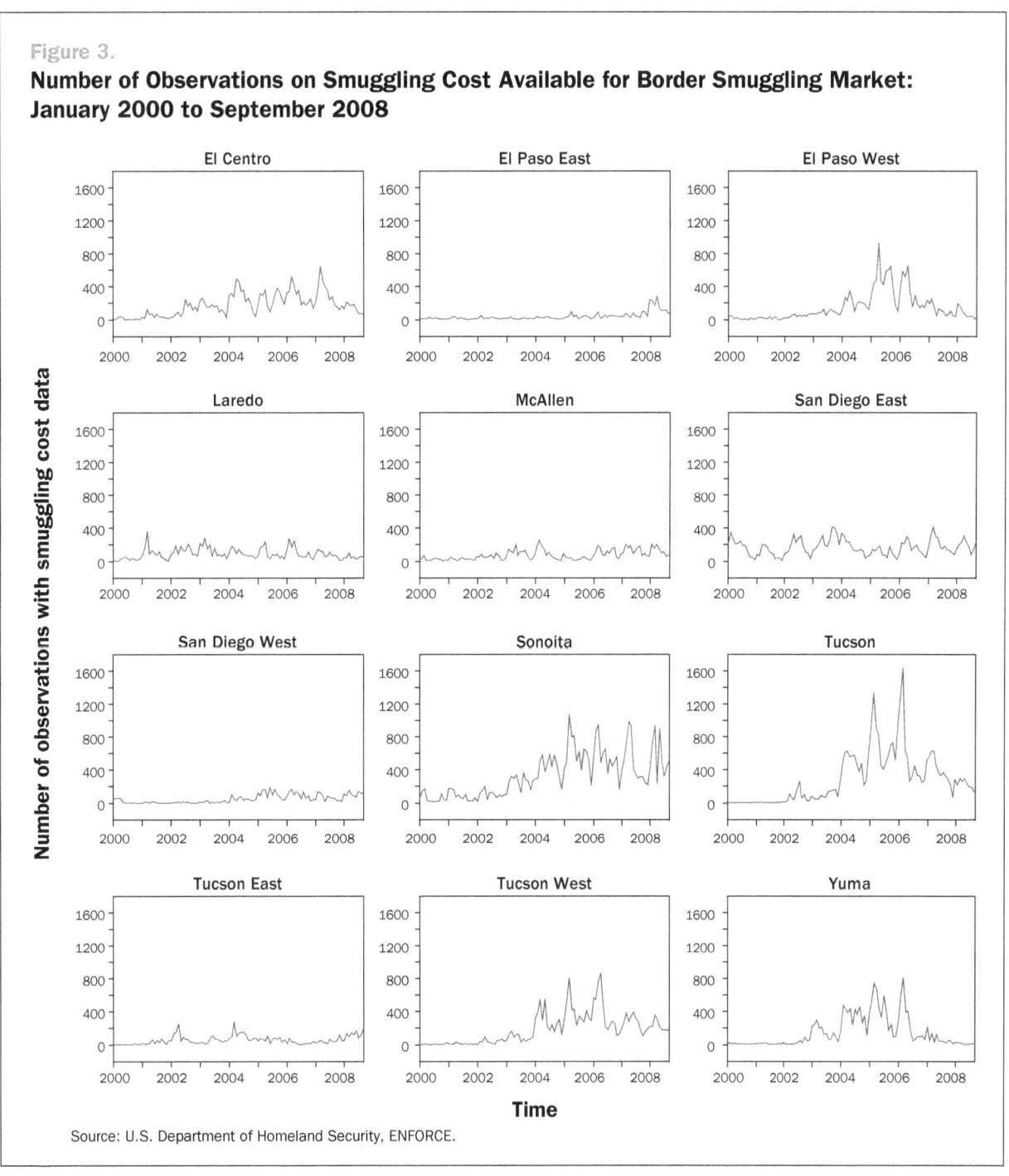

Figure 3.

Number of Observations on Smuggling Cost Available for Border Smuggling Market: January 2000 to September 2008

Source: U.S. Department of Homeland Security, ENFORCE.

To obtain a sense of the magnitude of crossing activity within the 12 smuggling markets, Figure 4 reports monthly apprehensions of those reporting being born in Mexico who were apprehended by Border Patrol at entry. To ease comparison across markets, for which the level of apprehensions varies widely, we plot apprehensions in log terms. Tucson is the market with the greatest number of apprehensions, followed by Tucson East, El Centro and Laredo. While Sonoita, San Diego West and Tucson show rising apprehensions over 2002 to 2008, there is no clear trend for Laredo, El Centro, or San Diego East. The series are clearly volatile, with pronounced seasonal movements and multiple spikes and dips.

The variation in apprehensions across locations is in part reflective of changing enforcement activity across Border Patrol stations. Figure 5 plots monthly enforcement hours by the Border Patrol over the sample period. Over 2002 to 2008, enforcement rises sharply in El Paso East, El Paso West, Sonoita, and Yuma, but remains more or less flat in El Centro, San Diego West, and Tucson East. In the 1990s, prior to the time period under study here, enforcement ramped up to push illegal crossing out of border cities and into more remote areas such that in the 2000s, intensification of enforcement

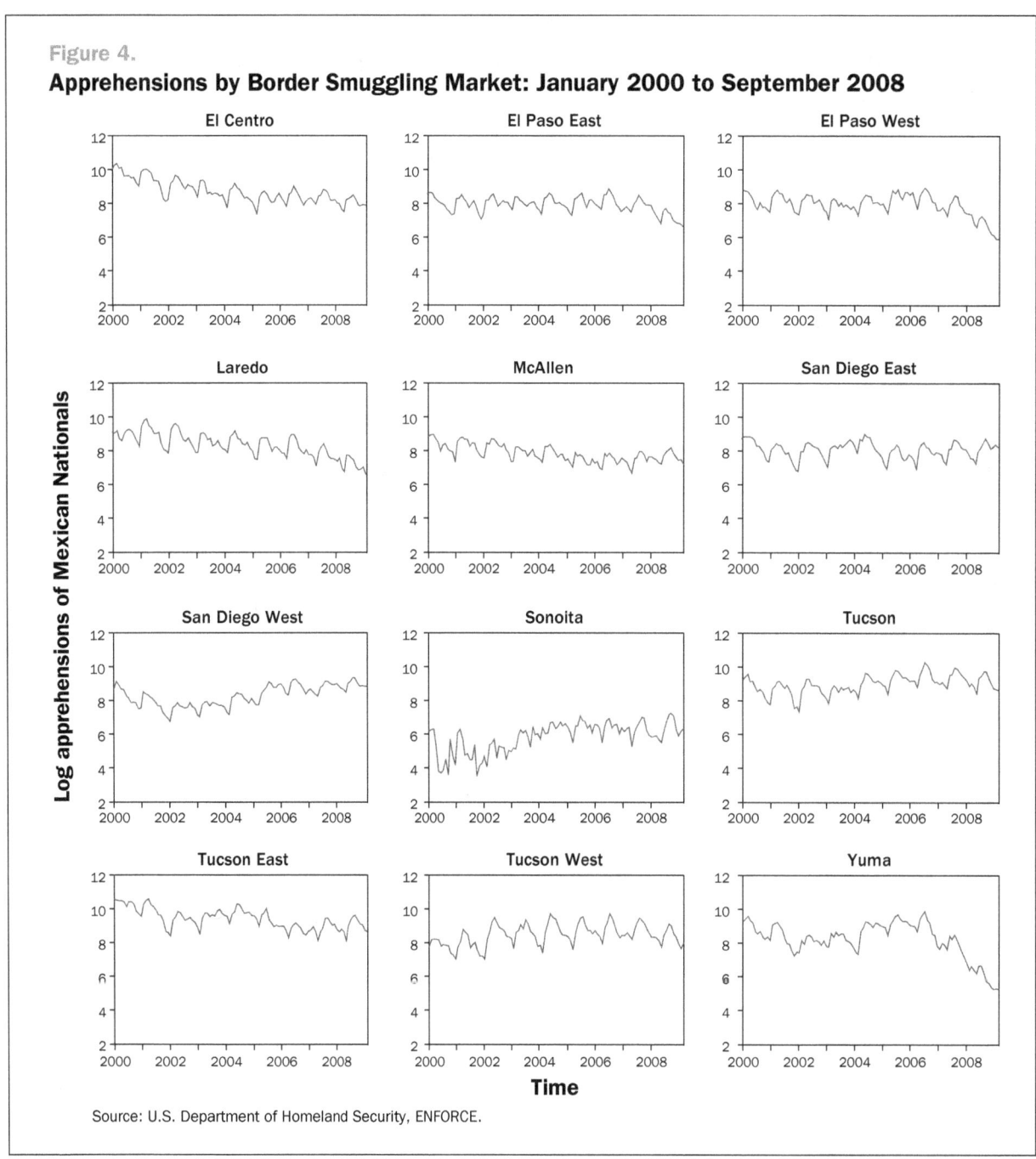

Figure 4.

Apprehensions by Border Smuggling Market: January 2000 to September 2008

Source: U.S. Department of Homeland Security, ENFORCE.

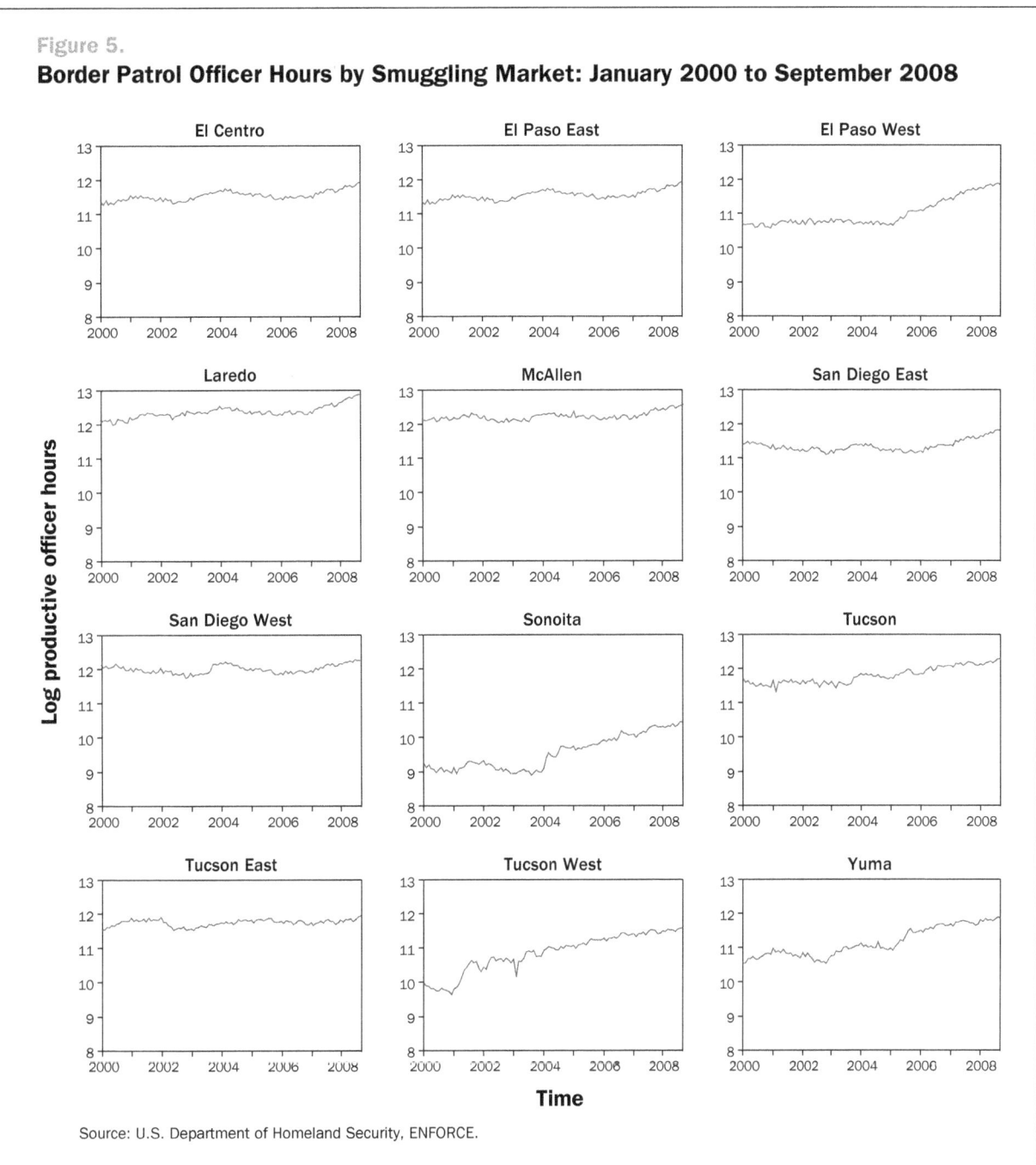

Figure 5.

Border Patrol Officer Hours by Smuggling Market: January 2000 to September 2008

Source: U.S. Department of Homeland Security, ENFORCE.

was focused on the more remote areas to which crossing had diverted. This variation in enforcement is helpful econometrically for identifying its impact on smuggling costs. Were enforcement to show a common time trend in all locations, its effect on smuggling costs would be impossible to separate from the trend. That enforcement rises in some places but not others gives us the potential to capture how changes in its intensity affect the price that smugglers charge.

The final piece of data we need for the analysis is the smuggling price. Not surprisingly, the price series are noisy, with some individuals reporting values that are either too small or too large to be credible. We trim the data by dropping the highest and lowest 0.5% of smuggling cost values from each smuggling market in each month. However, we report estimates for both the raw data sample with all the observations and the trimmed data. In addition, we also adjust the prices to control for any differences in reported smuggling costs associated with demographic characteristics (age, gender, whether they are travelling with children), place of birth (with individuals from traditional migrant sending regions in Mexico potentially having access to better information about how to negotiate smuggling markets), and season (with demand fluctuating according to weather, the agricultural growing season, and the seasonal construction cycle). Prices are also likely to vary by the composition of the group that is crossing together, with larger smuggling groups possibly obtaining group discounts but very large groups facing a price penalty owing to the difficulty in moving a large number of individuals across the border. Fortunately for the analysis, the Border Patrol records an event number with each individual apprehended that identifies all individuals in an apprehended group. We can therefore determine the number and characteristics of other migrants with whom an individual was caught.

To remove price variation from the data associated with individual characteristics, group characteristics, and seasonal factors, we run an initial regression of the log smuggling price for an individual on dummy variables for age and gender, variables measuring the composition of the group with which an individual was apprehended (fraction female, fraction children, dummy variables for the size of the group), dummy variables for the individual's state of birth within Mexico, and dummy variables for the month. We define the residuals from this initial regression as the smuggling price series "adjusted" for seasonality, demographic characteristics, and group characteristics. In the empirical analysis, we report results using three smuggling price variables: the raw series, the trimmed series (with the highest and lowest 0.5% values dropped), and the adjusted series (the residuals described above).

Figure 6 plots the trimmed smuggling price series (in log terms) for the 12 smuggling markets in the data. Each price is the average across individuals apprehended in a given smuggling market in a given month (we log the smuggling cost for individuals and then take the average across the logs). It is clear that the smuggling price is very noisy for the markets with relatively few observations (El Paso East, McAllen, and San Diego West). The volatility in the series declines after 2002, after which the number of observations rises (with the volatility decline being particularly notable for the larger markets, El Centro, Laredo, San Diego East, Sonoita, Tucson, and Yuma). Despite the differences in volatility across markets, they share a similar upward trend in smuggling prices over time, suggesting that different geographic markets are linked. Here, we see additional evidence of the upward trend in smuggling prices associated with rising enforcement. Rising enforcement at particular points along the border appears to have put upward pressure on smuggler prices across the border.

Before proceeding to the empirical estimation, it is useful to identify the variation in smuggling prices that we will exploit in the analysis. As we have mentioned, prices in a given smuggling market will be affected by average prices across markets and overall economic conditions in the United States and Mexico. This sensitivity of smuggling prices to overall border conditions makes it important to control for general macroeconomic conditions, otherwise we might attribute movements in smuggling prices to enforcement that are in fact due to other factors. Recognizing that there may be many unobserved factors that affect the smuggling market, we "dummy out" aggregate conditions by including dummy variables for each time period in the estimation. With nine years of monthly data on 12 smuggling markets, we have 1,296 potential observations. Controlling for time period means including 107 (9*12 − 1) dummy variables in the estimation. Referring back to Figure 6, the component of variation in smuggling prices that we exploit is that which is idiosyncratic to individual smuggling markets. The time period dummies remove time trends and other movements in smuggling prices that are common to all locations. Importantly, this means that we are controlling for change in economic conditions in the United States and Mexico that are systematically impacting smuggling cost across all smuggling markets (see footnote 5 for further discussion.) The remaining variation is that which is unique to a smuggling market. In the estimation, then, we examine how changes in enforcement that are specific to a particular market (and not part of an overall border buildup) affect smuggling prices in that market.

Further, to control for unobserved factors that are specific to individual smuggling markets, we express log smuggling prices in first differences (which removes the market "fixed effect" from the data). We include in the analysis dummy variables for each smuggling market. With smuggling prices in first differences, smuggling market dummies control for time trends that are specific to each market.

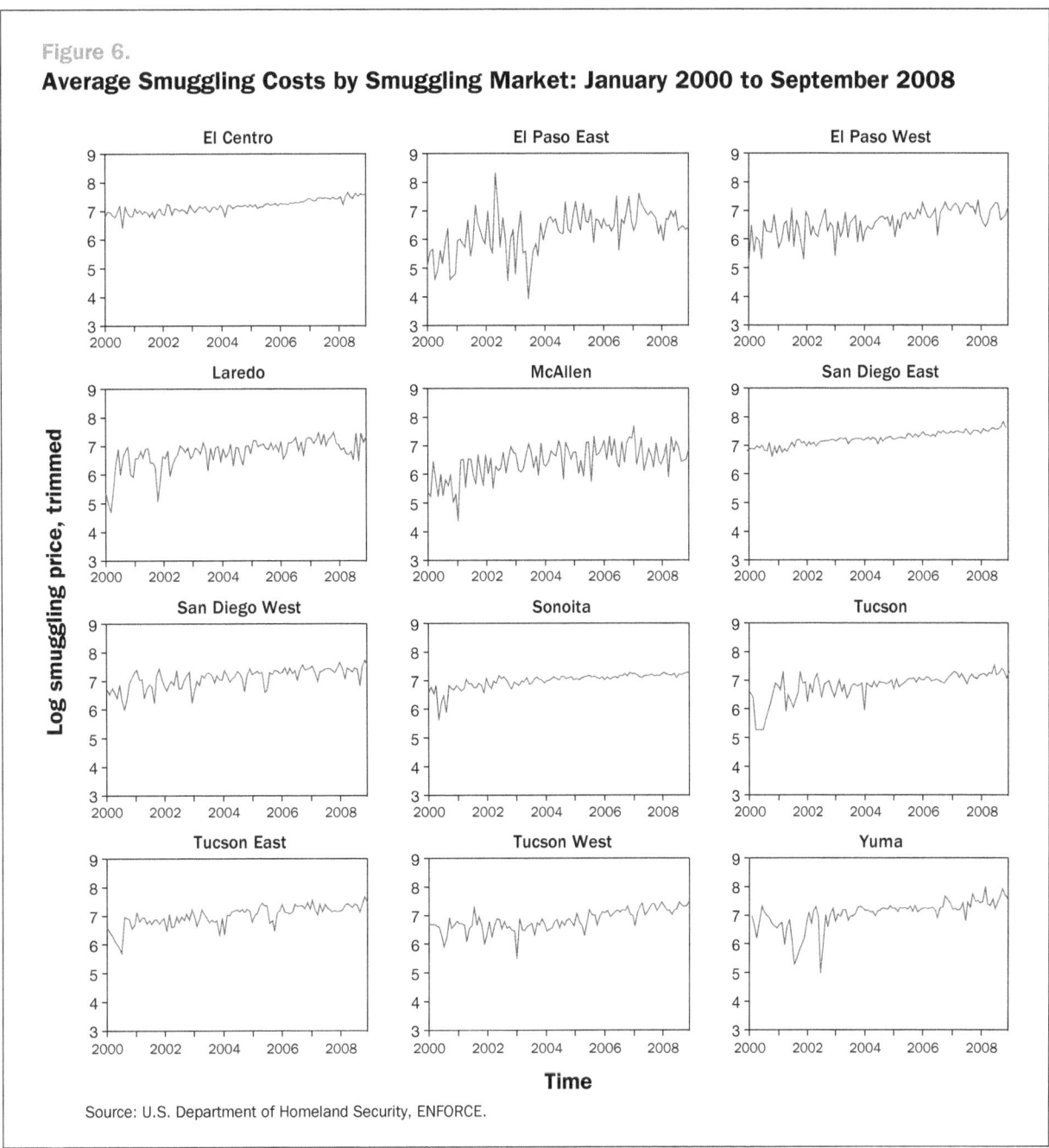

Figure 6.

Average Smuggling Costs by Smuggling Market: January 2000 to September 2008

Source: U.S. Department of Homeland Security, ENFORCE.

Estimation Results

The econometric estimation consists of regressions in which the dependent variable is the change in log smuggling price in a smuggling market and the key independent variable is the change in log enforcement hours in a smuggling market. A smuggling market binary variable is included that is equal to 1 for the smuggling market where the price is reported and equal to 0 where the price is reported for a different smuggling market. A binary variable is created for each smuggling market to control for differences among smuggling markets not related to enforcement hours. Month and year binary variables are included to control for changes in demand and supply for smuggling services that would vary over time, but not vary by smuggling market (e.g., economic conditions in the United States or Mexico, the seasonality of migrations, or the average level smuggling prices along the border). Later, we report results in which we include additional control variables in the estimation.

Table 4 reports the estimated coefficients on enforcement hours for different model restrictions. We estimate regressions for three smuggling price variables: raw smuggling costs, trimmed smuggling costs with highest and lowest 0.5% of values dropped, and trimmed smuggling costs adjusted for seasonality, individual characteristics, and smuggling characteristics as previously described. The raw data exhibits the most variation in reported smuggling prices and the adjusted series exhibits the least variation. The component of the variation that is attributable to noise in the data and not the true variation in prices reduces the relative importance of systematic variation in the regression variables and tends to reduce coefficient estimates in absolute value (i.e., it biases them toward zero). Consistent with this tendency, in virtually all regressions the coefficient on enforcement is largest for adjusted smuggling costs, next largest for trimmed smuggling costs, and smallest for raw smuggling costs. We focus on results using the adjusted price series as we believe this series contains the most systematic variation in smuggling costs.

The estimation in Table 4 also restricts the analysis to the post-2001 sample. Rows (i), (iii) and (v) estimate the model for the time period 2000 to 2008. However, since smuggling prices are sparsely populated in the data before 2001 and the limited observations increase the noise in the prices as evidenced previously in Figure 6, rows (ii), (iv) and (vi) exclude this period and estimate the coefficients using the post-2001 sample.

Finally, the estimation in Table 4 considers different weights on different smuggling markets. The unweighted coefficients reported in rows (i) and (ii) put equal weight on each smuggling market. The sample size-weighted coefficients in rows (iii) and (iv) weights the total elasticity of smuggling price with respect to enforcement by the sample size of smuggling prices reported in each smuggling market. The apprehension-weighted coefficients reported in rows (v) and (vi) put more weight on smuggling markets with more total apprehensions and put less weight on smuggling markets with less total apprehensions to determine the effect of enforcement on smuggling prices.

Table 4.
Estimates of Elasticity of Reported Smuggling Costs with Respect to Enforcement

Row	Smuggling cost sample	Adjusted, Trimmed Sample	Trimmed Sample	Raw Sample
(i)	Unweighted Sample	0.528 (1.96)	0.505 (1.78)	0.379 (1.13)
(ii)	Unweighted Sample—Post 2001	0.560** (2.19)	0.552** (2.13)	0.373 (1.10)
(iii)	Weighted by Sample Size	0.350** (2.26)	0.328** (2.08)	0.343 (1.88)
(iv)	Weighted by Sample Size—Post 2001	0.371** (2.33)	0.339** (2.15)	0.317 (1.70)
(v)	Weighted by Number of Apprehensions	0.340 (1.14)	0.350 (1.14)	0.218 (0.61)
(vi)	Weighted by Number of Apprehensions—Post 2001	0.656** (2.58)	0.631** (2.44)	0.478 (1.45)
Observations		184,953	184,953	186,643
Controls		Market, Month/Year, Gender, Age, Group, Birth State, Inverse Mills Ratio	Market, Month/Year	Market, Month/Year

NOTE: Parameter values are reported for the elasticity of border enforcement on smuggling costs for different model restrictions. The first column reports the estimates with smuggling prices adjusted to control for gender, age, group size, group composition, seasonal differences and the migrant's birth state. The second column reports the estimates with smuggling prices unadjusted by the control variables, but with smuggling price outliers trimmed. The third column reports the estimates with the raw smuggling prices. Rows (i), (iii) and (v) report the coefficients for the entire sample. Rows (ii), (iv) and (vi) exclude the sparsely reported period before 2001 and report the coefficients for the sample post-2001. The unweighted sample is reported in rows (i) and (ii) with an equal weight of the enforcement effect for both frequently crossed and infrequently crossed locations. The weighted estimates by sample size are reported in rows (iii) and (iv) with the enforcement effect weighted by the number of observations in the sample. The weighted estimates by sample size are reported in rows (v) and (vi) with the enforcement effect weighted by the number of apprehensions reported at each location. T-statistics in parentheses, robust standard errors used, ** significant at 5%.

The baseline coefficient reported in row (i) of the first column is 0.53, and is statistically insignificant at conventional levels. This coefficient is the elasticity of smuggling costs with respect to enforcement, or the smuggling cost enforcement elasticity. This estimate is for the time period 2000 to 2008. Dropping the first two years, the smuggling cost enforcement elasticity rises slightly to 0.56 and is statistically significant. The larger coefficient estimate and smaller standard errors are consistent with an increase in the number of smuggling cost observations in the later sample period. A value of 0.56 indicates that when enforcement increases by 10%, smuggling prices rise by 5.6%.

These two initial regressions are unweighted. That is, the unit of observation is the smuggling price in a smuggling market where all markets are given equal weight. Figure 3 shows that the number of observations on smuggling costs differs sharply across markets, reflecting underlying spatial differences in the number of individuals attempting entry. Because smuggling costs are an average across apprehended individuals in a market, it makes more sense in statistical terms to weight observations by where migrants are observed crossing the border. The estimates in rows (iii) and (iv) in Table 4 weight by the sample size of reported smuggling prices in each smuggling market.

An alternative weighting methodology is employed in rows (v) and (vi) where the coefficients are weighted by each market's share of the total number of apprehensions along the Southwest border. The number of apprehensions in a market during a given time period is an appropriate weight if the number of apprehensions is an indicator of the "true" number of migrants that enter through a particular market and if the observed average smuggling cost was an unbiased estimate of the smuggling price for this population.[25] Using apprehensions as the weight, the smuggling cost enforcement elasticity is 0.34 and is not statistically significant for the 2000 to 2008 period and 0.66 and statistically significant for the 2002 to 2008 period.

Which of these estimates are most credible? The unweighted results are the least credible as using average prices without adjusting for the sample sizes on which these averages are based is difficult to justify econometrically. Proper methodology when using average prices would suggest one should use sample-size weighted regressions. As it turns out, the results are sensitive to the weighting scheme used. For the post-2001 sample, the smuggling cost enforcement elasticity is 0.36 if weighting by the number of observations in the reported smuggling price sample. On the other hand, the smuggling cost enforcement elasticity is 0.66 if weighting by each market's share of the total number of apprehensions.

The only other smuggling cost enforcement elasticity reported in the literature is that estimated by Gathmann (2008), who obtained a value of 0.25. Our results are between 50 percent and more than 100 percent larger than hers. The differences could be the results of either data or methodology. We use monthly data for 2002 to 2008 with smuggling costs collected by the Border Patrol. Gathmann (2008) uses annual data for 1968 to 2003 with smuggling costs based on retrospective surveys collected by the Mexican Migration Project).

Our elasticity estimate of roughly 0.35 can be used to evaluate the overall impact of the border enforcement buildup in 2006–08 on smuggling costs (as measured in DHS apprehension records.) The change in both unweighted and weighted mean log smuggling cost is .115 for 2006–08 and .279 for 2004–2008. The change in log aggregate enforcement (sum of productive hours by border station and then averaged across months within a year) is .318 for 2006–08 and .372 for 2004–08. Using an elasticity value of 0.35, the change in enforcement hours accounted for 97% (.35*.318/.115) of the 2006–08 change and 47% (.35*.372/.279) of the 2004–08 change. We thus conclude that the increase in enforcement on the Southwest border accounted for all of the increase in smuggling costs in the period 2006-2008, but only about half of the increase during 2004–2008. This can be explained by non-enforcement factors increasing smuggling costs during 2004–2006.

---

[25] For reasons explained earlier, there is reason to believe that smuggling cost values in DHS apprehension records might be biased downward.

Extensions

We proceed to extend the empirical analysis in several directions. First, the specification we estimate is very simple with little in the way of dynamics. It may be that increases in enforcement take a while to translate into changes in smuggling prices as it may take smugglers time to learn about changes in enforcement activity. To allow for such dynamics, we experimented with including one, two or three lag changes in enforcement as regressors. In all cases, the contemporaneous change in enforcement retained statistical significance but the lagged terms were jointly statistically insignificant.

Second, while the time period dummy variables control for overall economic conditions in the United States and Mexico they do not control for differences in conditions that prevail among local labor markets along the border. For instance, when labor demand increases in Texas relative to Arizona and California the number of migrants seeking to cross the border in Texas may increase, leading to higher smuggling prices in Texas markets relative to other locations. To capture variation in local labor markets, we constructed a variable that is the average weekly wage for production workers in manufacturing, which is available at a monthly frequency at the level of US states. Many illegal immigrants work as production laborers in U.S. manufacturing plants in the food products and apparel industries (Passel and Cohn, 2009). We matched state wages to the border markets in which they were located. To allow for dynamics in wage impacts, we tried specifications with zero, one or two lags in the log change in weekly wages. In all regressions, the changes in log weekly wages were jointly statistically insignificant. We obtained similarly insignificant results when we replaced weekly wages with weekly housing starts in U.S. border states.

Third, we included the change in log enforcement hours for border markets that neighbor a particular market. Changes in neighboring border enforcement were statistically insignificant. This result may be surprising in light of Gathmann's (2008) finding that enforcement in own and neighboring locations affect smuggling costs. Recall, however, that by including time period dummy variables we have a far more extensive set of controls in the regression.

V. Conclusions

The cost of an illegal migrant being smuggled into the United States is a potentially useful indicator of border enforcement performance, because a rise in smuggling costs could indicate that enforcement measures are making it more difficult and costly for smugglers to successfully get illegal migrants across the border. U.S. immigration authorities have cited increasing smuggling costs as evidence of enforcement effectiveness in the past.[26] However, rising smuggling costs could also indicate increased demand for smuggling services whose supply is limited, or changing characteristics of the marketplace such as the formation of cartels by smugglers. This study uses DHS data and econometric techniques to isolate the impact of enforcement activities on smuggling costs as compared to other influences. Resulting estimates shed light on the impacts of historical border enforcement buildups and can be used to inform analysis of prospective enforcement buildups. The estimate of the cost elasticity with respect to enforcement of this study is consistent with an estimate resulting from a previous study that used a different source of data on smuggling costs. The two results taken together suggest that this elasticity has a value in the range 0.25–0.38, so that a 10% increase in enforcement as measured by Border Patrol hours causes smuggling costs to rise by 2.5–3.8%. Results also suggest that during 2006-2008, the increase in enforcement on the Southwest border accounted for all of the increase in smuggling costs, and in 2004-2008, about half of the increase in smuggling costs can be attributed to increasing enforcement.

Of course, the deterrent impact of this increase in smuggling costs induced by enforcement can only be assessed if an estimate of the migration elasticity with respect to cost is available, and this elasticity is challenging to estimate. The focus of debate on enforcement impacts should therefore now focus on whether the migration elasticity with respect to cost is significant, and acquiring the data necessary to estimate this elasticity.

---

[26] See, for example, Spener 2001, p.148, for an example.

APPENDIX: DATA SOURCES

DHS Apprehension Records

Starting in fiscal year 1999, the U.S. Border Patrol (USBP) created an electronic record of each individual apprehension made by a USBP agent. Individual apprehension records contain demographic information on the person apprehended such as gender, age, country of citizenship, and (if a Mexican national) state of birth. The records also include information on where the apprehension took place, including the Border Patrol station it occurred in. A fingerprint identification number is recorded that uniquely identifies the individual and enables identification of individuals who have been apprehended more than once. Apprehended individuals are also asked if they were smuggled into the United States. If the response is yes, an effort is made to verify whether the response is accurate, and how much was paid as a smuggling cost.

USBP apprehension record data on being smuggled and smuggling cost are subject to potential sources of bias. Apprehended individuals often have incentives to not report being smuggled to Border Patrol. Smugglers do not want to be identified because they potentially face prosecution. Clients who have a personal relationship with a smuggler due to being in the same social network or from the same home town may be less likely to report being smuggled. Clients of smugglers who have the ability to retaliate for being reported may have strong incentives to avoid reporting being smuggled. Because of such incentives, the reporting of being smuggled and smuggling cost to Border Patrol may be made unusually often by clients of abusive or incompetent smugglers who do not have any underlying social relationship with their clients. If these smugglers are systematically more incompetent than the average smuggler, then the smuggling cost that they charge might be systematically lower than the smuggling cost charged by the average smuggler.[27] Low rates of reporting being smuggled and smuggling cost may also be influenced by the fact that if a Mexican national reports being smuggled and a smuggling cost, they might become a material witness in a case against their smuggler, in which case they will not undergo voluntary departure but be detained to testify at a trial.[28]

There is also significant variation in the percentage of apprehension records that contain a smuggling cost value. Apprehensions reporting a positive smuggling cost as a percentage of total apprehensions are generally low and range from 1.0% in 2000 to 7.2% in 2008 (these report rates imply 16,750 and 50,507 positive smuggling cost observations respectively.) The report rate varied significantly across BP sectors and stations. In 2008, for example, the sectoral report rate ranged from 2.8% (Yuma sector) to 17.1% (El Paso sector), and station report rate ranged from 0.0% (several stations) to 80.8% (Sonoita station.) Although there is some stability in sector or station report rates across time, there is also significant variation. Variability in report rates may be due to collection practices of the Border Patrol, whose agents are not required to obtain a smuggling cost value from an apprehendee. Agents in some stations may go to greater lengths to obtain smuggling cost values for operational reasons particular to that area, or because management in that area emphasizes smuggling cost data collection for some reason. Behavior of those reporting smuggling cost values may also contribute to variability in report rates, as some locations may have a larger percentage of apprehendees who are more likely to report a smuggling cost than other locations. However, it seems plausible that report rate variability is largely driven by variability in Border Patrol collection practices.

---

[27] Figure 2 in the main text suggests that this might be the case, as the DHS average smuggling cost is systematically lower than the MMP and MMFRP series. However, the DHS and EMIF series are quite close to each other, and these series are based on samples that might be less selective than the MMP and MMFRP surveys.

[28] On the other hand, depending on the factual circumstances of the situation, an illegal immigrant who is the victim of a crime or who testifies in the prosecution of a smuggler may actually be eligible for an immigration benefit such as a U visa, and this would encourage reporting of being smuggled.

DHS Enforcement Hour Statistics

The traditional measure used to capture the intensity of border enforcement by the U.S. Border Patrol (USBP) is linewatch hours, which is the number of hours spent by USBP agents patrolling the immediate border area. The linewatch hour category was one of a number of administrative categories for USBP enforcement activities that was used in the PAS data system that was established by the legacy Immigration and Naturalization Service in fiscal year (FY) 1992. USBP reported to the PAS system through FY 2004. Other hour categories used in the PAS system included hours worked on interior patrol, traffic checkpoints, train and bus checking, and a range of other categories associated with supporting direct enforcement operations. In 2005, USBP ceased to report to the PAS system, but in 2004, USBP began to use a payroll system from which hours can be extracted. Hour categories in the payroll system can be broken down into "productive" and "nonproductive" hours. Productive hours in the payroll system correspond closely to total hours minus leave and other "unproductive" hour categories that were recorded in the PAS system. Because USBP reported to both the PAS and payroll systems in 2004, a comparison of hours reported to the two systems at the level of stations and sectors can be made. This comparison shows that although the levels are not identical, they are close enough to validate linking the two series and using the linked series for research (details are available upon request.) These series include linewatch hours but also all other "productive" hour categories reported in the PAS system, including interior patrol, traffic checkpoints, etc. Because linewatch hours account for a majority of hours worked, and particularly for stations that are on the SW border, inclusion of the non-linewatch hours categories should have little or no material impact on results.

Mexican Migration Project (MMP) Survey

The MMP survey has been implemented since the 1980s and randomly samples households in selected Mexican towns and villages in December and January of a given year in order to compile basic social and demographic data on a household, a year-by-year history of the household's migration to the United States, and detailed information on the household head's most recent trip to the United States. Two to five Mexican communities are surveyed each year, with 200 households typically being surveyed in each community. Following completion of surveys in Mexico, MMP then conducts interviews in the United States with 10-20 households whose heads comes from the same communities and who have settled in the United States and no longer return home. Surveyed communities have clustered in the traditional migrant-sending areas of Mexico.

Mexican Migration Field Research and Training Program (MMFRP) Survey

The MMFRP survey has been administered since 2005 and is based in three Mexican migrant-sending communities with different historical migration trajectories: Tlacuitapa, Jalisco (2005, 2007, 2010), San Miguel Tlacotopec, Oaxaca (2008), Tunkas, Yucatan (2009). The survey collects social, demographic and migration history data for nearly all adults in the community between the ages of 15 and 65 and similar data from migrants that reside in the United States who were born in the surveyed community. The typical number of responses for the survey in a given year is 700 to 900 responses in the Mexican community and 100 to 200 responses in the United States.

Encuesta sobre Migración en la Frontera Norte de México (EMIF) Survey

The EMIF survey has been implemented since 1993 in 8 Mexican cities near the U.S. border. A sample of people returning to Mexico from the United States is interviewed extensively about their migration and work experience. Information on documentation status in the United States is collected and how entry into the United States was achieved. If a person entered illegally, they were asked if they used a smuggler and if so, the cost of being smuggled. A total of 50,667 interviews were conducted during 1993-2005, of which 3,269 reported a positive smuggling cost (roughly 250 per year.)

REFERENCES

Andreas, Peter (2001). "The Transformation of Migrant Smuggling Across the U.S.-Mexican Border," in David Kyle and Rey Koslowski, *Global Human Smuggling: Comparative Perspectives* (Johns Hopkins University Press.)

Angelucci, Manuela (2005). "U.S. Border Enforcement and the Net Flow of Mexican Illegal Migration," IZA Discussion Paper No. 1642, June 2005.

Carrión-Flores, Carmen, and Todd Sorenson (2006). "The Effects of Border Enforcement on Migrants' Border Crossing Choices: Diversion or Deterrence?," working paper.

Comptroller General of the United States (1976). "Smugglers, Illicit Documents, and Schemes are Undermining U.S. Controls over Immigration," Report to the Congress by the Comptroller General of the United States.

Fuentes, Jezmín and Olivia García (2009). "*Coyotaje*: The Structure and Functioning of the People-Smuggling Industry," in Wayne A. Cornelius, David Fitzgerald, and Scott Borger (eds), *Four Generations of Norteños: New Research from the Cradle of Mexican Migration* (La Jolla: CCIS-UCSD).

Gathmann, Christina (2008). "Effects of Enforcement on Illegal Markets: Evidence from Migrant Smuggling Along the Southwestern Border," *Journal of Public Economics* 92(10–11): 1926–1941.

Hanson, Gordon and Antonio Spilimbergo (1999). "Illegal Immigration, Border Enforcement, and Relative Wages: Evidence from Apprehensions at the U.S.-Mexico Border," *American Economic Review* 89(5): 1337–1357.

López Castro, Gustavo (1997). "Coyotes and Alien Smuggling," in Mexican Ministry of Foreign Relations and U.S. Commission on Immigration Reform, *The Binational Study on Migration Between Mexico and the United States, Volume 3: Research Reports and Background Material*, pp.965–974.

Orrenius, Pia (1999). "The Role of Family Networks, Coyote Prices and the Rural Economy in Migration From Western Mexico: 1965–1994," Research Department Working Paper 9910, Federal Reserve Bank of Dallas.

Orrenius, Pia and Madeline Zavodny (2005). "Self-Selection Among Undocumented Immigrants from Mexico," *Journal of Development Economics* 78(1): 215–240.

Passel, Jeffrey S. and D'Vera Cohn. 2009. "A Portrait of Unauthorized Immigrants in the United States." Pew Hispanic Center.

Spener, David (2001). "Smuggling Migrants Through South Texas: Challenges Posed by Operation Rio Grande," in David Kyle and Rey Koslowski, *Global Human Smuggling: Comparative Perspectives* (Johns Hopkins University Press.)

Spener, David (2004). "Mexican Migrant-Smuggling: A Cross-Border Cottage Industry," *Journal of International Migration and Integration* 5(3): 295:320.

Spener, David (2005). "Mexican Migration to the United States, 1882–1992: A Long Twentieth Century of Coyotaje," Center for Comparative Immigration Studies Working Paper no. 124

www.ingramcontent.com/pod-product-compliance
Lightning Source LLC
Chambersburg PA
CBHW081819280526
45789CB00008B/3148